SLEEP WATCH

Sleep Watch

POEMS BY

Richard Tillinghast

WESLEYAN UNIVERSITY PRESS
Middletown, Connecticut

Acknowledgement is gratefully made to the following periodicals, in the pages of which some of these poems were first published: *The Atlantic Monthly*, *The Boston Review*, *The Carolina Quarterly*, *Fire Exit*, *The Georgia Review*, *Harper's Magazine*, *The Harvard Advocate*, *The Island*, *The New Left Review*, *The New Republic*, *Partisan Review*, *Poetry*, *The Sewanee Review*, *Shenandoah*, *The Southern Review*, *The Tennessee Poetry Journal*, and *The Yale Review*.

Library of Congress catalog card number: 77-82546

Manufactured in the United States of America

FIRST EDITION

The Wanderer rests in a shelter.
He obtains his property and an ax.
My heart is not glad.

This describes a wanderer who knows how to limit his desires outwardly, though he is inwardly strong and aspiring. Therefore he finds at least a place of shelter in which he can stay. He also succeeds in acquiring property, but even with this he is not secure. He must be always on guard, ready to defend himself with arms. Hence he is not at ease. He is persistently conscious of being a stranger in a strange land.

—I Ching.

CONTENTS

PART ONE

The Creation of the Animals

We were angels before the sky lost us
When it happened I touched myself
My hands were new   were not hands
We spoke sounds that no one understood
that were no longer words

He would come and watch our mouths learning the food
he gave us   in love with his own brilliance
Using his power had left him innocent
and he thought he had made us from nothing
not missing us   not knowing he had blundered
and we had fallen from the sky like tiles from a mosaic
never dreaming his strength
had struck out beyond his will

Later on   when he saw that things had gone wrong
beyond his power to restore them
it rested him to look at us
And I found I could love him in his weakness
as I never could before
The beauty left his face   and his eyes began to cloud
with the grief that killed him

I ran on the grass   made paths through the woods
felt the rain in my fur
Remembering the golden cities no longer moves me
I begin to forget   I flew once   and knew the order
of a beauty
I no longer have the mind for.

Water City

You are all I've thought of since I got here
      you know
In the dripping shirts that I wash
Your brown fingers in the suds   cheeks flushed
laughing at things I said
Let's forget the years in between I say
I would say

I love you
And this is true in its way

      You are
in my bed in this city
The sheets are flannel, boarding-house sheets
You are becoming all the women I ever love
We hear the rain   float to the far edge of sleep
The years come to my door
and knock and walk away sighing

What of the nights I lied to you
My hands are full of water   What
can I say   I
talk   afraid of my impulses
But you are your ghost now   the angel of yourself
Years between us

You can't hear me   Listen to
me   The years are raining
filling the gutters in Sussex Gardens   Listen to
the rain   the gardens   the years
You are a mere girl   washing your hair
telling me about the Pacific Ocean   Eucalyptus leaves
It's been too long

Sleep, angel Take back everything you gave
You've been with me too long

Naps

Leaving the alluvial city
when clerks were napping in the fly-blown hockshops
we came by boat to a deep bay
where sunlight gleamed on the brittle water
A hawk folded and was dying down the wind
Before his wings changed we dove side by side
I watch the water break from your arms
   sliding away

I feel the breathing
the air shrinking in my body
Then I breathe out the last of it
And it no longer matters
We are too deep to care

For seven nights
I have come to this city
crossing from the new quarter to the old
by a certain routine they carry out
   without my knowing
It is never as I had remembered
Smoke pouring from ships in the harbor
   blowing always
    into the old city stuffing the cries of the water-hawkers
People are rising to meet it drinking it into their lungs
as it draws them above the domes and minarets
The doorways and well-heads are covered with a script I have never
I have never seen before Yet I understand at a glance
the hawk the crocodile the fox-headed god
   Never as I had remembered

I let it go
out of my hands
You start to move
I kiss your face as it loses the dreams

Dreams of other nights
are something from another life
    To wake like a mummy in the dead light
    words falling from the ceiling
    like snakes through rotten plaster
    Always the same solutions
Something from another life

The first sounds are the children playing   hopscotch   jumprope
    all their games

Ascension Day: Waking on the Train

The soldiers always sleep erect
as though in training for an awkward death
Time and again they are there
when you wake from nodding

And your dreaming eyes find them
They are guarding you against threats of violence
But your cries do not disturb them
when you are carried off
Only the single round of the firing squad
                                        stirs them

Too late for you

Or the compartment is sealed   a tomb
carrying the war-dead home
You are there by mistake

Then the windows are full of the countryside
and animals know daylight for the first time
But after the commuters
cigars   windows being jerked open
your body begins to know it hasn't slept
It thinks of all the parts of itself
that would touch a bed   all the ways
It knows
a riverbank nodding with wild bluebells
Cattle low on the pasture path
Sunlight at the edges of leaves
is a golden blur   like the buttered toast
in pictures of healthy children

Could you sleep   fall through the sunny darkness

You see the earth begin to curve at the edges
People are reaching up for you
a balloon with no string   you shudder and wobble
Blue and green become one color

—I'm unhappy all the time   That's all
　Can't help it
—What can I do?
—Oh nothing   You can't do anything
　I'm a lost cause
—Then it hardly seems worth while continuing
—Yes I suppose you are right
　You are always right

—It's to be an erection   I mean ascension
　I should say the two are connected
　The man in the train compartment is to have an erection
　which in turn will cause the giant balloon to ascend
　Quite a stunt

—But my sister and I have been here
　since this *afternoon*   Why dudn he hurry?
　Cain't you see anything from where you're standing?
—There seems to be some delay   He's
　gotten part of the way up   but seems to be
　hanging there   just above the ground

The hands take the laundry off the line
pull you into the windows
The firing squad is in position
They bring you down with one shot

"Ladies and gentlemen,
there will be no ascension today."

The mind of a man in a warm room
      A lion
    pawing the memories

       If I raise my window
the girl across the street is playing
the piano   Chopin   Mozart sonatas
The easy ones

        I used to watch
    the rain   the wall flowers
    bloom inside out   clouds faces tigers
    Come into the room Mother
    Sit at the end of the bed

The kitten
    watches my secondhand go round
      paws my turning pages
Am I playing with her
    or she with me?

Outside I knew it was winter
The room got cold so fast
I didn't see
the flowers wilted
I can't remember what happened to them

A lion stalks me through the
ruined flowers   I pity even an insect
caught by a bird

Come sleep   Come hours   Come days

Dozing on the Porch with an Oriental Lap-rug

The aging pederast my friend
badgers me
to sign away my dead aunt's auctioned house
                The screen goes black
The screen   I remember   I am awake on the sun porch
Chilly   and the tide is going out

Lotus blossoms   pears   the Indian ram
All the symbols   I can never remember what they mean
Every year the sea makes the rug forget
something of what it means

Whatever I was thinking whatever I was
dreaming about   nothing but dust and cinders
Old leaves

I let it go knowing only
it is four in the afternoon
a cold June so far
Cold enough for a fire

All day my head has been floating
above me
I am modest about it
What if one could would one sever
all connection with the body?
Favorite theory of mine
I am in love with my thinking

Slowly the weaving   the lotus blossoms
tide going out
snuffs out the borders   erases the screens

Sycamores and sweetgums losing leaves
this early   and the chestnuts
going yellow
It was summer when I
came into the park

It seems so recently
we were walking from my office
Smell the rain you said
It's Spring.
Then I was putting in the screens.

What has happened
to turn my mind to trivialities?

I can only think about
it
by switching my eyes from this bench
to a vacant one
telling myself that is how
it would look if you
were dead now

I have left for work early
stunned at being awake
dazed and heavy with breakfast

I try to imagine the absence of you
Light on the wide sheets
no breakfast sounds in the next room
while I may sleep late

No sounds
but those I think
are in the next apartment

La Vie Littéraire

Surly, unambitious
the flies languidly
loop the loop near the porch ceiling
It is what passes for
Spring here

Picturing Nancy at work
her arm
inside the glass case
reaching for pastries
the customers point to

I push back the afternoon's responsibilities
mend a screen
Anything
to make her think
I haven't lolled the day
away
watching TV
doing the crosswords.

Anthropological studies
tell us:
In some societal setups
(e. g., Oceania)
the women do all the work

Men of superior
talent and training
should spend their time as I do—
metaphysical speculations,
literature.

This Is Final
to Leslie

What with everything
up for grabs   winner take all
7 days a week
Explanations   (subjective-objective)
The city down in the mouth

What about those of us thinking of you
Your adolescent premeditated elegance
imitating I decided later a movie star
        (Ingrid Bergman?)
Or recurring glowing and dazed among the
dreamed sheets

Not knowing I had these things
These are things I keep
And it is always you
in my
"Let's move into the other room"
my Keats-over-Wordsworth
my serve and backhand
whatever

What do these things mean
now in our in-every-way dispassionate
seeing each other maybe once a year
in our independently cakewalking
towards twenty-five
then thirty

When I remember
how your mother
cried a little
on her fortieth birthday
with all of us there

Someone walked over her grave.

The Silent Bride

Meeting my college friend's new wife   Women
I woke up saying in my sleep
should be seen not heard

Why should our mouths become electronic
devices to
square and cube
talk
Language is not coconut
to be hammered rubberly,
drained and grated
Not repellent to be sprayed at nervousness

Shhh

Quiet

It is cold snow in our faces
while sea turtles rise along our shores
The pan of milk puffing to a boil
in our forgotten kitchen

We drove for miles across three states
ears blanked by the rush of the windows
We loved the black and white articulation
of drive-in movies we could not hear
And in the morning
slow blankets of sunlight repeatedly falling

Recruited by my father
I raked romantically
as more leaves fell around me.
They bundled in my arms
        being of one substance with the air,
drifting in the heaped-up gutter.

My father set the pile ablaze
and tended the ragged edges
in a flannel shirt and sleeveless yarn pullover.

His blue-grey
incorruptible eyes
blinked
as the smouldering leaves plunged and
settled in the waver of air.

I watched him growing comfortable
with the blurring remnants
praising me
and yawning
as the hazy afternoon fell round about him.

Mirror, Mirror

1.

I am whatever you are.
Be yourself,
Dance as you wish
before me . . .
the fair flesh rising
meeting its special shape
in my imagination

2.

Is that all you got to show
for yourself?
Cut it out
junior!
We've—all of us—
seen your kind before.

I wanted to get you a picture of the room
where the two of them sat always
in the dimness of things: the windowseat clouded
by a shorted lamp, the samovar
thick with tea, outdated railway passes
catnip mouse, books piled against the nailed-up door—

Those were some of the things. One of them would strike
days off in bunches, always behind, remarking
"First day of winter," "President Harding
born, 1865." The other one
would sometimes weep over the spectacle, and check
lists arranged for errands repeatedly begun.

Sometimes when water trembled in the drains
and drugs or lack of supper burned the world's dust away,
they saw things their way till the yellow day
and wandered the elated gardens. But mostly
the cat crumpled cellophane
and someone went down for groceries.

No mail came, no offers. Stories below, pedestrians
inched their way antlike through snow that fanned
the vague streetlights with a flutter and stabbing stroke.
No one came stamping through the door, up stairs
and trembling corridors to where
they sat smoking and dazzling the room with talk.

Reading

A low nasty day
perfectly still
my eyes became to slip
through holes between words
in the alleys running
from line to line like snail tracks.
I am afraid to tell
It have been on my mind a week now.

How many winter mornings waking wrongly
at three or four
my mind the only luminosity
in the darkened house . . .
Covered,
my wife richly breathes
her eyes turned deeply in
on dreams.

I am alert at once
and think of the cat
coasting on its muscles
from closet shelf to bureau
grave and all-seeing
caring not at all.

The face   the faces
waiting
toward ponds
empty-handed and with tenderness
hoping the hourly day might melt and flow
One could reach out—
there might be a daily salvation

Out the windows slowly
a dull light is covering the
world without end:
snow patches and mud ruts,
the neighbor warming up
his car.
The world refuses
to bless
or to be blessed.

The Keeper

Our animals are sleeping.
The eyes of the dog move dreaming his paws
shuffle feebly
about his nose,
And the cat's long sleeping noise
so low as not to be heard, and treble.

I drift in the chair drowsy
while the others are sleeping,
a family
drawn up in their beds and cozy
their future devolving on me
as a kindness—the one who answers, the keeper.

Rain on the pavement and roofs of sheds.
One thinks of bluegills slurping gnats
and little frogs among the lily pads.
Time lapses impossible to picture
the dial of a clock existing anywhere
except perhaps

vastly
the numerals curiously wrought pale green
against the stars The hands glide into vision
now here now there and scarcely
give the appearance of motion
describing an imaginary plane.

I stare
no farther than my glasses The mirrored eye
looks through lidless having no lash of hair
Behind the glassy sky
it never closes or opens, and keeps
us. It neither slumbers nor sleeps.

1.
The essence of gasoline is in the streets.
Plastic china is on sale, and cars full of chihuahuas.
In the house with telephones,
no one can see beyond the windows
where taxis cruise,
their headlights mooning on our ceiling
like aquarium lights.

2.
Behind these things   beneath the voices at a fire
is an engine cutting down   all vibration
the pistons lapsing in their cylinders.
Inside all radiators—   the dripping and knocking—
ignoring the stone dome of resonance
where leaded metal sloshes deeply,
must be such a passage as this:
green, inarticulate, subterranean—
seals ducking in and out the waters,
brighteyed fish breathing upward.

Quieter than the paths of a formal garden,
quieter than a map of New Hampshire,
is this falling off.
We wonder about nothing that does not smooth our eyes.
Here is a single tulip alone, and red.

Impenetrable darkness—
when you pass your hand before your eyes,
there is not even the illusion of sight.
The extinguished lamps are left behind—
one moves by touch
through the narrow sandstone tunnels.
When our cat was gone,
I heard her drowned voice everywhere
crying down the gently sloshing paths of stone.

3.
Miles above is the real
sea   and a happiness we never know—
the happiness of ants on white paper,
the mind pliant
like blank film lying in solution.

Green water   blue water
the bubbles surfacing like marble.
Patterns like smoke rising in a cobalt sky.
Yet they are flat, and sway gently for miles around the ship—
a brightness coming off the air.

At night,
in the ocean night
when ever so briefly
we break the water—
        down paths of bluish fire
        through clouds of invisible seaweed,
the terrible phosphorous rising for the moon.

Less Than Yesterday, More Than Tomorrow

Rising from sickness
my bones thin, bending, tender to the touch,
a lightness in the inner ear

Things seem to rush at me.
I huddle away from them, my mother driving—
the street is shocking to the wheels.

They are solicitous, the potted plants
lean towards me, older.
I can see what they were thinking,

They thought . . .
The smiling nurses smiled and looked in all directions
when I was shaved, a necktie, erect on my feet.

Now for a while I possess this room—
the sofa and the fire are mine, lighting the fire
is totally my province.

The floor floats, at sea.
In the window glass lake water, dry leaves floating.
The globe is out of date.

Less and less I feel I am falling forward.
My mother is less patient,
my father will send me to Florida.

For them I am closing the door to the place
where the dead children are stored,
where the pets have gone to Heaven.

The End of Summer in the North

In country churches sheaves of wheat are brought in.
Flowers are laid in the whitewashed sills of the deep windows.

As is decent,
the old and sick are taken driving in the country,
afghans and sweaters over their knees.
They praise the sunlight glowing about them through the glass.

Cottage gardens they have never seen before.
Sunflower stems sag helplessly beneath the enormous blossoms,
huge dahlias blur their eyes with unheard-of brilliance,
and even the late asters are not homely.

In their cities
people are glad for small favors.
They crowd the parks and spread out over the grass.
Or in an outdoor cafe, patient with a slow waiter.

A week of rain will kill it,
yet the kitchen-help and shop-girls are laughing
through the big square
going home from work in the rain.

They clack their umbrellas along the fence
of the closed amusement park,
and peer through at the rides and concessions.
The boarded windows of the dance pavilion highlight and gleam
like patent leather in the rain.

They see themselves inside still,
as they were,
faces glowing up from the new lagoon
floating beside the upside-down pagoda
and the ghostly painted paper lanterns.

too fidgety to include
Jane Austen,
too fatigued and changing
to write these letters
my handwriting veers around the upright.
I put the cap back onto the pen
the way a court reunites a
mother and child.

Around us there are sleeping
families   Heads of families
snore beneath plaid lap robes

We are best
seen in terms of our cars
facing forward   the children in back
limited by the glass, locked in by the doors.

Our cars are together
in the hold of the ship.
They crouch together bumper to bumper
like cells in the deepest part of the hive.
The rubber tires grip
the car-deck.
The metal bodies tilt
when the ship rolls in the winter weather,
the springs and shock-absorbers
shift in their clear grease
with intense precision.
Those well cared-for move in silence
in a still place under the heart of the ship
as she rolls in the arms of her winter lover.

Goodbye

for Bob Grenier

When they would wake me before I wanted to
wake
at eleven, the knife-grinder
insisting I shake hands
with someone called "Rhino"

Kept reaching for my watch
Kept losing my ring
Kept diving for my money—
In my inner ear
the long diesels bore down
on New Jersey.

What I loved
was standing at the edge of the subway dock
with trains cascading into the station—
to float for a step or two in the roar
as it carries me off my feet.

Mr _____ was arrested in the lobby
of the fashionable
soaked with
reading a paperback
inside the black room
(where he was not a guest)

Now it will surely happen
Nothing further to
Wrap him!   not my
—Knocking the faces off, all
over now.

and sleep
in a single breath
the length of the darkness.

Things are
as you remember them—
a calf drinking milk that sloshes through a sieve
a cat running down a well
ferns growing through a roof.
You can hear a leaf
scrape
down the road forty feet.

Everything is wood smoke
and the smell of planked fish.
The fire logs hiss
into the river.

Our shoes are muddy
from when we fed the horses—
wifely, uxorious
they steamed in the March air
as they turned away toward the forest.

My hands are so cold
I hope you can read this.

(for Luke Myers)

"Come Home and Be Happy"

1.
Before I know it is there at all
it is all around me.
It lays its hand
on the water in the public fountains.
The air darkens
and a chill goes round my shoulders
like a shawl.

What form will it take for itself
Water running   horses swimming
a flight of birds   a bell   a tower
something that moves in three parts
and turns round on itself?

I sit like this and liken it to a spirit
striking and striking at the whirling void
for entrance.
I start to move
like particles in the field of a magnet.
The buildings radiate,
the broken glass is singing in the street
"Come back to me and be happy"
it is saying.
It takes me by the arm across years of the closing day
as I run along a grassy ridge   pretending that I am a pony.
It is the time when the long lanes of cars
are switching on their lights—
the rows of white in one direction, and the rows of red.

It is leading me through a storm of oblivion
making my eyes bright with the knowledge
of rooms that no longer exist—
where the yellow shawl before the gas-fire
is keeping the bed from bursting into flame.

The old woman with her whooping laugh
is forcing scrapbooks into my hands.
"You are a true".. etc.

2.
You find yourself
walking
without intention
playing a certain set of streets as a standard opening
or closing . . .
You are drawn past
rows of little shopfronts closing
·library assistants making arrangements for supper
parlors being lighted   arms reaching up to close the curtains

The two of you are standing in a rainy field.
Someone watching says aloud
"This is the most beautiful thing I have ever seen"
(the old Budweiser horses?)
She bows her head slightly, steaming in the rain
and starts to walk across the field,
the great hooves graceful as snowshoes in the slush.
You are proud of her beautiful fetlocks
trailing their silky hair in the wet,
as she dreamwalks in the marsh.
"I wear her like a legend round my neck"
you think
"I will be a cowboy unicorn and squirm at her feet."

At last you enter.
Knowing your shape the walls contract around you.
This is home, she is here.
Wherever you step you inflict a comfortable pain.
Love is real—and you have done the work yourselves,
haven't you—
papered the place in fur.

The Same Bird Again

Sunbathing near sleep
on the fast deck of a tacking sloop
the voices of pretty friends around us
mindless   like bright scarves
If only we were happy   this
would be our happiness

Beyond the blue of the sea there is no blue,
it eludes us simply.
In my hand
I feel time turning to its opposite.
Yet for a few moments this morning you . . .

Topless, oozing tubes, tears,
the sound of crystal
shattering
the hesitant depressed monotone . . .

I float in the water and watch you floating
near me
like a stick of wood.
You can see what we have built—
the horizon
drifts,
lemon groves, luxury hotels, the arrow cypresses
going up into the mountains. . . .

I don't want this
ever to end.

quand du Seigneur,
from the forest without chairs,
the lost father submerged among the living,
       my dreary enchantment,
the child's photo   scared eyes
one sees every day
mirrored

to the shared nowhere of this room
your room like a treehouse
warm with you in the eye of our first storm,
the high trunks elated in the wind,
snow blurting girlishly off the roofs—

Submerged, alone,
in the common water and air,
through the eye-struck pool-mirror we gaze,
Narcissa-Narcissus.

Are we the two fish
of my dreams, sleeping in motion
side by side, cruising
together, helpless?

Will they bury us together?

IS

That is who this

is

Who

is   this

that   is

"Everything Is Going To Be All Right"

This in no way involves calling
the cat you call "Lady"
(and having her come). Nor
cruising the leafy side streets filled with girls,
checking out every one for the one
face . . .
Years ago, lonely for fun
you would stroll and peer into those intelligent interiors
thirsting to penetrate that domesticity—
the white walls, the art books to the ceiling,
the candle for lovemaking . . .
Now that is what you have lived.

The bus that takes you
where you want to go,
where does it take you?
Home to the joys of home,
the daily surrender to being loved

While you were working the blizzards moved in and kept
        streaming past the windows
while slowly you made your living by talking.

No one's around—
you leave and
as though the city were a map tilted on its
side you follow all directions
the way a marble does

To swim in air as snowflakes,
as fish swim in water!—
rising into the midst of brightness
into the snow falling since morning

Snow-mole, headfirst
in the easy, first drifting
feeling the slope coming up to meet you
teasing to spin out
Fine snow ticking into your eyes
out of control
into the drift
iciness
eating your pulse
then just falling, soft
falling   through the clouds
Did she mean to start you in this
something you lost how long ago?   shadowing
through the deep-tunnelled streets
where you first lived—

Is everything sliding?
Nothing
to worry about—
Getting lost means sliding in all directions.

A Letter

(about Piero della Francesca's portraits
of the Duke and Duchess of Urbino)

Was Piero's Duchess of Urbino spoiled
when Berenson used her
for his cover?

He didn't. That's by what's his name   Pollaiuolo.
The impression, though, surfaces continually
as the blue of their sky
becomes in depth the blue of my wall
where they confront each other daily
when the room starts with light
(almost hear a radio)

What did they lack that you and I lacked?
His pose
turning the one unravaged cheek to the artist—
suggests a dignity
we easily find too easy.

Even the well-made bed
of Berenson's description—
"The artist, depicting man disdainful of the storm and stress
of life, is no less reconciling and healing than the poet who,
while endowing Nature with Humanity, rejoices in its measureless
superiority to human passions and human sorrows."
          —a different world.

There's a simpler way to say this
one feels,
as I lie in the dark and drive myself
to examine my notion of your conduct—
"if she could do that then,
            then
(biting the hand she forced to feed her)"
my limbs neck pillow
like motionless Aztec sculpture
weigh down in their stone solidity . . .

Our life, all the grace of a record-changer . . .
But was there a time—
so different from these nights—
we moved together as we wished
like remembering music?
All I wanted
was music that could care for me.

The landscape background, is it something they wish?
Through hills that float like clouds
in the cloudless sky,
the low walls keep out no one.
The breeze that moves the small boats
over bottomless clear pools
wishes to suspend us forever.
In the washed air attending their impossible heads
nothing could hold us back
from floating in the world of their grace—
radiant as the three pearls of her tiara,
empty as the clear Murano beads she wears.

PART TWO

I

Leaving with the others   so bright was your picture of the room
you hadn't even noticed the taxi
until it was
simply another way of doing the walls,
a portable room—
Those tricks of vision—   the "million points of life"
New landmarks   and the willingness of time
to become very slow

That fast drive along the beach road
She was driving
The little car seemed to hold to the road by an effort
of engine noise   sliding
on turns where sand fanned over the asphalt
You hardly knew where you were
Coming out of the smoker
onto the swaying place between cars
you grasped the rail and let it shake you deeply
Was it the coast?   they were working at night
building ships
arc-lights flaring   the blue blinding torches showering sparks
into the ocean

                    Arriving
in a part of town mostly deserted,
the little one and a half storey stucco duplexes
Depression style
Someone hammering   at a great distance
the far-off rhythm of cars going through the gear-shift

Moving by instinct
inside the Moorish gate
the constant giggle and shouting of the blacks
red-headed   brilliantined

Past gossamer cotton candy sellers
the dated and suicidally rickety roller-coaster looping
in the figure of infinity over a marshy field,
scarier in the daytime than at night—
Past people shooting the heads off moving Japs
Past the crazy mirrors
stretching you between feet and face until you break

Into semi-darkness   the Old Mill
where the boats rock there gently
paint rubbing off them
water lapping over the wooden gratings,
an air of ozone

A man with a blank face sits   touching
some gear-shift levers   not moving
People begin to come into the boats
shyly   mostly in couples
some in groups of three.
We move from boat to boat
seeking the best spot,
my brother in the front seat.

A noise of gears
and the water is muscling and herding
the boats dipping headfirst and rearing
as they head for the tunnel

A last flash of sunlight
a presence as of simultaneous flashing
You pass through the hoops and rims and lips of yellow sun
rushing again and again monotonously into vision

Then the darkness
Steady water forcing the line of boats

wedging them to the side
Passages of solid blackness
like sailing through a cellar of coal
all sounds from outside cut off long ago,
the gunwhales barely skimming at times the walls
    Sailing smooth between the outside gunboats
    with no loss of steam   the men in high spirits
Trembling on the pulse of water
    with the Duchess swinging for the fourth time
    the champagne exploding in slow motion
    seeming to float in a highly organized cloud
    as the Dauntless . . .
Water quiet
    The sky turning red in the sunset
    the women waving their little arms like shrimp
Used to the dark   but seeing nothing
    Pointing the bow at the steady V of white water
    stones gushing all around
    When you try to turn it
    broadsides in white water
    C-stroke just in time
    to barely miss
    gashing the bottom on a stone
    The stern bounds   gives way
    to the current's rightness
    Water boils the packs out
    over the thwarts   the bailing can bobbing

    away   through the rapids
    Straight
    to the slick-rock bottom
    the green moss streaking past
    You manage to stand
    but the way a cardboard cutout soldier stands
    in a closet of toys   only moving
    trying to place your feet
    the breath gone out of your body

Straight through the dark

2

Why did we cherish those tunnels   those empty drainage pipes
my brother and I?
We knew the network—
the long ones under the golf course
the dark, diagonal one under the parkway
the tangles of brush   moss   highwater marks
of flood-molded hollow sticks and mud
the found golf-balls—
the flashlights   predawn campfires   cold chocolates
Whole days in this refuge
beneath the blazing streets of the city!

But the Old Mill was odd beyond our knowledge
built before anyone remembered
so variously reported
We could feel the deep vegetation sway beneath the rush of the boats
And there were tales of native animal life
Blind fish born white without any pigment
Dragonflies that could swim like crabs
Nails with eyes   Whole cats that glowed in the dark
Bats that curled themselves like mopheads
        and leaned in the corner
A lady in the form of a snake

Some rides were noisy
I liked the ones where nobody breathed
You could hear a pulse in the water   never breaking the surface,
at times the tiny and welcome rattle of oarlocks,
an almost imperceptible slush

as the foundation settled down
an inch and a half in bottomless mud

Bottomless River!
Idling   naked on a sandbar by the Mississippi
fingering a shell
hearing the heat-struck breathing of the mud-flies
the occasional boat whistle
and across the river the industrial closing bell
the air-raid siren every day at noon
the sand deliciously hot and yielding

3
This is how a leaf falls:
from as high as it has been
to as low as it goes
without choice   not knowing
Who are these people?   the spots of clouds
changing to different brightnesses
Fireflies swarming in the olive trees
What do these numbers mean   why do they go in a circle?

In a long hall I stood
at the first doorway of the lost life
The great creatures sitting rigidly   palms flattened on their knees
came toward me
the eyes impenetrable
the judgement of stone

Birds and fish became confused and cried aloud
I stood in flames
the world coming apart in my hands   the very arms and faces
coming loose from the colossal statues I adored—
Would I remember?
And yet my only thought was
"What is expected of us?"

4

And you this afternoon
you at your desk reading,
if I could set you free this afternoon
from the model of an Egyptian cat before you on the desk
from your likeness in the mirror
            bright and owlish with knowledge
from the woman asleep on the bed,
to leave your room by the window
above row after row of real   or pseudo-Georgian houses,
the parallels veering off and banking in formation
into a blue expanse and nothingness

What would you have seen   or remembered?
The cities built into the walls
coming around the corner in those delightful turns of vision,
A Swiss village on the mountainside   the same from year to year
radiantly boring?
or the Oriental city   my pure delight
the lighted pagodas and smoky domes and minarets
Or simply the horrors of your own dullness?

That precious dullness restoring control.

And on the way back, what does one wish for?
Happiness of some kind?
One wanted   perhaps   snow falling on the city
wetting the smooth stones
making the concrete glow and neon be terrific
Then feathery arcs around all lights
Great mittens of whiteness bending the evergreen trees
and hiding streams and paths
Everything still   springy   and balanced
like the branches of the fir

5
People sound cold down in the street.

And this is what one wanted after all—
to be lying in the room
however you wish to imagine it
the walls are blue   reflecting snow
and the Japanese lantern is swaying

You begin to stir and look around you
after twenty-four hours of sleep.
In another room are voices
faint   like the sound of water
barely trickling in a drain.
She is standing near the window
putting something on a plate.
Did you dream it   or did someone actually say?—
"You can wake up now   it's over."

PART THREE
1959–1963

Visit to the Peach Farm

for Henry Dalton

Two dressed in white in tall-backed chairs
Sit together to gather
The last sunlight of eighty years
The fading warmth of each other.

This kind of air meant peach weather
To him, and a sun-dashed roadstand.
Now it's hardly worth the bother
To up-reach to branch and down-bend

To basket. Now we come round bend
And down hill, surprised that neither
Regards us as close-enough kin
Or friend that he would not rather

Sit on the porch and not bother
To rise, white-haired, from his chair,
Idle in August peach weather,
To greet two from a strangely distant year.

Sea Cycle

Cold, cold five o'clock:
  The grey windows dawning.
Alone, I awake.

Night dies soon. It is
  Cold, cold. Five o'clock:
    The grey windows dawning.
  Alone, I awake
On a sea of days.

Again, though it does not matter,
  Night dies soon. It is
    Cold, cold five o'clock,
      The grey windows dawning.
    Alone, I, awake
  On a sea of days,
Bobbing beneath the black water.

Tomorrow light will flood the room
  Again, though it does not matter.
    Night dies. Soon it is
      Cold, cold. Five o'clock:
        The grey windows dawning
      Alone. I awake
    (On a sea of days,
  Bobbing beneath the black water)
No more: lost in the break-tide's boom.

Mid-morning, walking back,
I almost stumble looking down,
Watching the operation of my brown-
Shod feet, how they click and clack
On the sunny morning sidewalk. Soon
I will be at home; the buildings thin.

Beside the street a tree
Lies fallen. Mossy green and black,
The twisted limbs crouch dragon-like;
A redbird flits at me
From a branch, like a dragon's tongue of fire—
No Pentecostal fire-tongue for *my* hair!

Fifteen steps up the stair
To an empty room on an empty floor.
I yank open the bureau drawer,
Encounter the deadly glare
Of a Gorgon's head of twisted socks.
From the writing desk I see the cracks

In a casement-window pane.
My likeness splinters and veers in the glass
As the wind sways the window without cease.
Some sector of my brain
Tries the rest by calling up scenes
From memory and noting the response.

Bit by bit the sequence
Is shown. I stiffen in my chair
To watch the dreaded scenes, familiar
As movie plots to a child who frequents
The neighborhood movies. And then
It comes—the all-expected awful end.

Triolet

Sweep the soggy tennis court
And fill the empty swimming pool,
Red leaves of fall! Summer is short.
Soon the snow will, quick to start,
Sweep the soggy tennis court
All winter long till spring when we shall
Sweep the soggy tennis court
And fill the empty swimming pool.

To My Grandfather, Dead Before I Was Born
for Martha Williford Tillinghast

I have been, in the still afternoons of December, a child
On the floor in a room where the light was infused with a dust
Like the dust of mortality. Books from the high, glassed-in shelves
That encompassed the room were the source of the gold-feathered
    host

Of minuscule faeries escaping a leather-bound volume
When pages were turned. I have longed for a word from you, Sir;
I have let my imagination enquire what your thoughts
Might have been. I have hoped for a note on the margins of
    Shakespeare.

I have waded a quiet stream at the earliest hour
Of morning, when mist wound and circled the willow trees,
And the golden-backed bass shivered the water like spring rain.
I have settled a cast in the shadows. A bass would seize

The fly and go skittering sideways upstream to deep water,
Entangling the line in the rocks—an explosion of white
In the morning's first sun as he thrashed for an instant, then broke
Away, free from the barb of the hook, from my limiting bait.

The moment of contact has left my hands trembling. I reel in
The spiraled, limp line and resume the rhythmic casting.
You handled the tackle before me; I feel in the bamboo
The precedence of your fingers, as though they were resting

Around my own, imparting some secret knowledge,
As once in the attic as I was exploring with flashlight
I came face to face for the first time with you—high-collared
With bristling mustachios, silent in an oval-shaped portrait.

Quietest of all, I have stood at your grave with the family
And have looked at your weathering name and have seen the old
    holly tree
Finally wear out at the roots in your mound and begin to die.
I have wondered towards your spirit, Sir, past the roots of mortality.

The Moth and the Chandelier

A moth whirred through the window.
The chandelier on the ceiling
Was the main attraction,
Though the moon seemed full that night.
The brightness of the light
Took note of his affection
By etching the course of his wheeling
On the walls as a sputtering shadow.

Fluttering from his course
As the glittering chandelier
Was no longer a distant thing,
He spun against the wall map
Of England, with many a snap
Of wings, which slurred as if to sing.
He lost his footing there,
Shook backwards like a horse—

(A horse, perhaps, with wings)—
But lost this posture soon
And bumped into the plaster
Venus. Not meant to be wedded
With her, again he headed
Chandelier-ward, faster,
Struck this imitation moon
And died with electrical pangs.

The lamp still buzzes;
Its dull fluorescent glare
Makes windows opaque
To the dance of flurried snow in the outside air.
Frozen branches crack,

The falling snow hisses
Groundward in the dark.
Inside I read
Cold-blooded Dante, climb the stubborn peak
Which surely soon must lead

To Beatrice,
Or I must give it up.
On a page of notes
I sketch an imaginary girl with eyes as deep
And crystal as the moats

Of Paradise,
Her forehead high and clear
As Beatrice's.
And I find all that I ever want to love there.
Other eyes and faces

Look straight at you
And are too definite.
I want the snow to stop and let the moon
Fill up the night.
I want to run

Loup-garou,
Changing, screaming
Across the snow,
Feel growing tooth and fingernail becoming
Bloody fang and claw,

Hear the ringing
Echo of a scream
Born from the blood
Go rolling and sighing to the spring of a frozen stream
In a cave on the mountainside.

I find myself running
Up the attic stairs
To the roof to throw
La Divina Commedia over the houses and stars
In a sacramental vow

To leave home,
Books, everything.
I hear truck tires
Along empty highways droning their siren song
Of ultimate longs and fars.

It Is the Fourth of March Today

It is the fourth of March today
And may I say
I take it as the first of Spring.
I could be wrong?

I walked around all afternoon
But found too soon
My lungs were heavy, knees were stiff
From not enough
Walking and too much sitting and too many
Books and rainy
Mornings, and hardly any sun.

I wanted to throw myself to the ground,
And ring around
The rosies and make a daisy chain—
Do things I had done
As a child, when we would walk miles from our house
To see the first crocus
Blooming, in a child's green-and-gold land.

I don't know what I should have done
If Wordsworth had come
Walking by, with a slack daffodil
In his lapel,
Or God, walking in the garden.
"Beg your pardon,
Sir, for having all my clothes on"

Would be the thing to say to the latter
(As clay to the Potter).
I guess I should have reprimanded
Heavy-handed
William for picking the pretty flower,
For in an hour
He would have danced it to a tatter.

Poem

I read these poems over, hoping
To remember what I had expected
Of myself. You appear
On every page of words, reflected

As bright leaves are in an autumn pool
That laces itself with winter's color,
Till lately the unimaged leaves clatter
Darkly down on the sightless mirror.

The noise of my poems must needs be—
If you turn to them idly in a journal
Or find them filed in the memory of a drawer—
Brown, thematic, and unvernal:

An old song out of fashion, tinkling
In a music box when you lift the lid.
You had forgot the machinery was there
Or the name of the tune it played.

What I Write About Is You

I knock in from the elements' brawl
This hardest night of the fall,
Hands nervous over the latch-key
To a cold and empty house,
Thoughts stopped at an old impasse.
What I write about is you.

The sacramental agitation
Of the spheres insists relation
To my blood. Water is raised
And forced up rusty at the drain,
Guttering like plasma to the brain.
Lightning stammers, and the room is glazed

In unnatural blue. Leaves mix
In the dank and mouldy syntax
Of air, to spell a helter-skelter
Report. A cold crow caws from the grove,
Crying for warmth, not love.
The thorn trees offer little shelter.

I think of a night with you in a May
Field, dawn under a pear tree.
And I am undone. When a man and his house
Are shaken thus, what to say
Or do? Better to be
With the frozen crow in the thorn tree.

I Move in Love for You

to Suzy,

Girl of settings, of early morning,
I rouse today and move in love
For you, out of the tangles of sleep.
From drowsy bedclothes that have

Wrapped me in their woven limbo
And held me fast in darkness of dream,
I rise to consciousness from you
And waver on the rim

Of day, reluctant to shake your faint
Receding presence from my eyes
Which now adjust their range to view
The outer world and lose

This lingering insight into dark.
The windows show up slate-grey, dripping
Cold rain, and they must be closed.
Spattered screen and sopping

Frame give up a strong wet sting
To the smell of air. Birds are silent
Amid the huddled leaves. I breathe
The secret hush of the moment.

I touch my fingertips
Together and touch my lips, my cheek.
My finger-ends remember skin
Of your face, down of your neck.

Soft is the rain on leaves, but softer
Were your rain-wet lips when dawn
Surprised us early and we walked
Outdoors to be again

Surprised by the sleepy-headed drizzle
That settled itself down without warning
And shook the bright rain on your hair.
Do you remember the morning?

Daylight and its forms imposed
Themselves on us. Your patterns grew
In me as day enlarges out of dawn.
I move in love for you.

A Poem on the Nuclear War, from Pompeii

The August blackberries harden and sour.
Their vines rattle at a breath of volcanic dust
Through the portico of Juppiter Sator.

Plucked juicy from broken stone, the fruits suggest
A semblance of cycle. The principle could not be
More apparent; in the wreck of the past,

In the dead fusion of marble and lava, the seed
Of new greenness begins. But the berries sour on my mouth.
Hot wind and cinder sun have frayed

The vines and wizened the sweetness of the berries' growth.
Not only Pompeii, but all of Europe seems
To drowse here, dazed in the sun towards death.

It is a time of stopped time, when ruins
Of the human mind are tangled with stunted fruit
Of the future. A new sun blots Vesuvius—
Of earth and sky, the old, the new destroyer.

Let the boat luff, jib and main swing free.
Wind drops, wrinkling the green
Tide that shuffles down towards Capri
Burning yellow in the setting sun.
We yawn and stretch and talk of where we've been—
Been all over Europe, tired of the civilized world,
Tired and sleepy, rocking, peacefully lulled.

The US Navy jets drone over again,
Their vapor trails scoring the sky above
The old Etruscan fort set among green
Olive trees. The manic engines rave
And pop the eardrum of the sky as they dive
In practice at the harbor, wrenching sound from sight.
It is rehearsal for the death of light.

Our words hang up in the wind, fused by a flash
Of thought, and powdered dry. We are dumb
As Hiroshima, canceled in the hush
That follows the blast. We shall be made one
With the sea-sucked bones of dead sailors, Ulysses' men
Sunk in the Mediterranean storm—finger
Fused to finger in the neutrons' instant hunger.

If You Were Here

If you were here you would listen
To the thunder shudder like trunks
Being pushed across the attic
And turn aside from the window, as often
I have seen you turn in the static
Summer air before light shrinks
To a tangle of trees above the horizon—

Turn away and come to bed.
Now the rainy wind sways
The tree and speckles the dust on a packed
Box of books. The landlady said
It this afternoon with great respect:
The lady is leaving? The gentleman stays?
Now I have packed all I could,

I finish the sherry that would not fit
And wait for time to go to the station.
The blood and muscles have their reasons
For loneliness, who know by heart
The sacraments of your presence.
Wine brims to my lips in sad celebration
And the windows watch the night start.

A Lady's Song

What better place than a ruined garden
For a lady to mention her sorrow?
Crab apple is my fruit,
The yellowed Queen Anne's lace my flower.

When summer goes dry with middle-age
And the nights glaze shut with drought,
A bitch in heat howls on the ridge
And all the dogs turn out.

Rose flush at my cheek would blanch at a word
Of impropriety. Tiny veins
Would insinuate blue at temple and neck.
(Mother taught us to avoid scenes,

You must make them feel a lady's presence.)
My hand, sought after for years,
Was put to pouring at receptions.
I tremble going down the stairs.

September: Last Day at the Beach

A high blow tousled all the yachts
In the basin; green, yellow, and red shells
Bowled and whacked sides. The buoy bells
Scattered their moist petals into the air
And all up the beach the summer's gates
Were swinging shut. The wind smacked your hair

Onto your mouth, and all I now can see
Of your face is that you did not smile
At me. Even before the pale
Salt-wash flecked whitely at your ankles
Your name before my eyes ran grey.
I would not follow where the waves remold wrinkles

Of sand and drag the stem-eyed crabs
To dash on stones. I sat upon a dune
Watching you kilt up your skirts and frown
At the spray, thinking how after the dancing
And wine and kissing in taxicabs
You had come to me in the black of morning

Your damp hair braided like a child's,
Petal-sweet, and held with a rubber-band.
At rolls and coffee, when daybreak unwound
Us, we had talked awhile of staying over:
A walk on the beach would stay the pulls
Of plan, the tow of destination—
When we were two east-west trains in the station
Pulling apart, forever, forever.

If you love the body you must know the bone
that ribs and peoples it; deeper than flesh you feel
the beauty. That will last, simply as stone

upheaves in season where the winter rain
rakes asters and drooping cornstalks from a hill.
If you love the body you must know the bone

of fingers that touch, of the high case where the brain
lurks, of the deep knock and door and sill.
The beauty that will last, simply as stone

remains, is what you love when the blossom is gone—
petals and sepals and stem, roots and soil—
if you love the body you must know. The bone

smiles behind our faces when we frown,
knowing while the sweet flesh will not hold
the beauty, that will. Last, simply as stone

lasts, my love. For saying what I can
I ask forgiveness—in time we'll know it well.
If you love the body you must know the bone,
the beauty that will last simply as stone.

Enter Your Garden

Violent all day as a wind-tugged kite in a tree
my body rode it out—that single passion
chugging the heart like gin.
I got drunk on it, and all I could see
was parts of bodies flickering in my vision.
In the streets I dwelt on sin,
the subway was a tunnel of corruption.
I have made my bed
in darkness I said
And the worm is my mother and sister

Enter your garden or call it what you like
Your alleyway may buzz with garbage cans
You can be deceived
if you let yourself. It is easy to mistake
the smells of garbage, flowers, and your sins
Or is it only me?

This hour of evening all over the city men
are being unfaithful to their wives. The queers
in parks are doing favors
among the statues and cops; and the setting sun
is sin's color when the madeup queens and whores
wake up, throw off the covers,
remember who they are
and hit
the street.
We are faithful only to the beautiful

If at all. Going home I dream up
smiles and faces, make them grow on the unreal
subway riders, tell
them they live. If they could breathe they'd steam up
the crazy mirrors one sees them through. I feel
you turn to me as I come up
the stairs. Today's last film flaps off its reel
and as we fall asleep I waken, feel
you dreaming all the colors of our life.
And as the water truck whirrs by, you laugh.

For a Teacher's Wife, Dying of Cancer

Four-fifteen: a weak snow starts to blot
The city's likeness. I know you are dying.
By tonight chained tires will be churning it,
Headlights plunging into it. No planes will be flying
South from Boston. They will squat in rows
Staring at the snow that grounds them. The mewing
Sea-birds blown inland incuriously rise
Through it all, scorching the flurry with furious eyes.

Your dying glows in my brain: dry light spreading
Through the nerves, converting the cells like cancer
The crab, that pinched your lung once it set in.
I hear the lie scratch like an old record when you answer
You are feeling fine. On the phone your voice
Could almost be a ghost's, half-heard in the tense air.
I dream an ice-storm, poles crashing,
Hot wires sparkling where they loop and cross.

Down South it must seem warm enough for your walk
Today. When your husband asked us over for a drink
You would meet us in your funny walking shoes and sulk.
We talked the modern world to arm's length—
Fireside Agrarians; not even cancer
Could usurp the house's form. You shrank
From our courtesy to closet with the stranger
Whose passion banked your eyes of their gutted fire.

A man can't live in a house with death, your husband
Told me. We shooed the screech-owl off the roof.
But in this lying and cobalt time, when the doctor has been
Made a god, I had hoped to offer you truth.
The storm beats down the birds with an iron grace
And my warm words freeze and shudder in my mouth.
The snow swallows my reflection in the window-glass—
I can't remember your face.

Praise for a Household

Waking on your kitchen floor
I keep my eyes shut—nose
Remembering spice tins where they were
Last time I slept here—keep my eyes

Shut, and I lapse into the parlor
Where my mother kept an apple
Stuck with cloves: nose curler.
Even now the light floats supple

On your chairs, among the dishes
In the sink. No need to look,
We've never had a rainy morning.
The morning streams with goldfishes

Smiling in the placid light beams.
When I go to steal the neighbor's paper
The bosom-windowed buildings lour
Committee disapproval.

I cannot know what morning you two wake to
In your bed too narrow for any but lovers;
My bachelor dreams are none that would shake you
And start you wide-eyed from arms and covers.

Before life clamors at the door
Before the windows start to roar
I give you simply what I can,
The selfish praise of the single man.

The Beauty of the World

Where am I? The sleeping bag
Grapples my legs on the dirty floor.
When the sun at a window waters the smog
Before the conscious morning's dream,
A man is being sucked over Niagara
Falls trapped in a barrel. Then I am
The man, the barrel becomes a drum—

Not with rumbling we heard last night
When thieves ran down the street with stolen
Sheet-steel, but steam that made me sweat
In my sleep clanging up through the pipes.
I wake like a fevered child, the sweet
Hangover wine like cough syrup that creeps
A turpentine snake in the bronchial tubes.

When morning pumps into my veins
I feel the strangeness of it. I try
To go back where it all begins.
The recollection floods my heart
Like snakebite—the venom of hating one's friends
That swelled through dreams in the dark
Possesses me in every part.

In many ways there is no place to go
From a friend like you. I look down
At the slum backyards frothed over with snow
And think of the boy with the octopus brain
Floating pale and wavy through
The murky waters of Schopenhauer
While your mother wheedled by the hour

"Come down and mow the lawn Ted. *Please.*"
Unhealthy even in the summer
I breathed the airconditioned days
In Memphis and swallowed your conversation
Like the bitesized crustless sandwiches
My mother fed her mah-jong "girls".
I struggled to bridge these worlds.

I leave without trying your door, and lapse
Into the city like a second sleep,
Like yellow ether-dreaming, maps
Of anger fretting the roof of my sight
And vanishing. Dry-humored friendships,
Noble in reason, do not delight
The sounding shark, a prince in his watery night.

Distinguished contemporary poetry in cloth and paperback editions

ALAN ANSEN: *Disorderly Houses* (1961)

JOHN ASHBERY: *The Tennis Court Oath* (1962)

ROBERT BAGG: *Madonna of the Cello* (1961)

MICHAEL BENEDIKT: *The Body* (1968)

ROBERT BLY: *Silence in the Snowy Fields* (1962)

GRAY BURR: *A Choice of Attitudes* (1969)

TURNER CASSITY: *Watchboy, What of the Night?* (1966)

TRAM COMBS: *saint thomas. poems.* (1965)

DONALD DAVIE: *Events and Wisdoms* (1965); *New and Selected Poems* (1961)

JAMES DICKEY: *Buckdancer's Choice* (1965) [National Book Award in Poetry, 1966]; *Drowning With Others* (1962); *Helmets* (1964)

DAVID FERRY: *On the Way to the Island* (1960)

ROBERT FRANCIS: *The Orb Weaver* (1960)

JOHN HAINES: *Winter News* (1966)

EDWIN HONIG: *Spring Journal: Poems* (1968)

RICHARD HOWARD: *The Damages* (1967); *Quantities* (1962)

BARBARA HOWES: *Light and Dark* (1959)

DAVID IGNATOW: *Figures of the Human* (1964); *Rescue the Dead* (1968); *Say Pardon* (1961)

DONALD JUSTICE: *Night Light* (1967); *The Summer Anniversaries* (1960) [A Lamont Poetry Selection]

CHESTER KALLMAN: *Absent and Present* (1963)

PHILIP LEVINE: *Not This Pig* (1968)

LOU LIPSITZ: *Cold Water* (1967)

JOSEPHINE MILES: *Kinds of Affection* (1967)

VASSAR MILLER: *My Bones Being Wiser* (1963); *Onions and Roses* (1968); *Wage War on Silence* (1960)

W. R. MOSES: *Identities* (1965)

LEONARD NATHAN: *The Day the Perfect Speakers Left* (1969)

DONALD PETERSEN: *The Spectral Boy* (1964)

MARGE PIERCY: *Breaking Camp* (1968); *Hard Loving* (1969)

HYAM PLUTZIK: *Apples from Shinar* (1959)

VERN RUTSALA: *The Window* (1964)

HARVEY SHAPIRO: *Battle Report* (1966)

JON SILKIN: *Poems New and Selected* (1966)

LOUIS SIMPSON: *At the End of the Open Road* (1963) [Pulitzer Prize in Poetry, 1964]; *A Dream of Governors* (1959)

ANNE STEVENSON: *Reversals* (1969)

RICHARD TILLINGHAST: *Sleep Watch* (1969)

JAMES WRIGHT: *The Branch Will Not Break* (1963); *Saint Judas* (1959); *Shall We Gather at the River* (1968)